The Cycle of a Flower
By Lizy J Campbell

*Dedicated to my love
who consistently inspires me
to write and be true to myself
'Your Smile' is
exclusively you.'*

We were meant to Grow; but I will remain always me…

GROW

Just like a seed that sits in wait

In darkness and despair

Thinking this is life with no light or air

Laying untouched and broken

A small hidden gem, it does not know

Waiting for the earth to shift and shake

The soil to loosen, the feel of the gentle strands of sunshine up its shell

Gaining strength, endless energy to thrive

Striving to find the highest point, craving to spring roots deep

It breaks ground, head held high

Its fears diminished now tall and proud

Taking in rays of nurturing sunlight, its stem and roots strong

It grew despite darkness, in strength we grow

To thrive in joy

JUST ME

But I am just me

I am flawed, headstrong

I don't ask for help

Every time I do

Inside my head deemed vulnerable, weak

I've gone through hell

Picked up my self-worth and shattered heart pieces off the floor

I intimidate

Act like I need nothing or no one

Full of thorns

But in every sense of the word love, I wish to be it

To have someone who can understand

To embrace all of me

Perhaps my life is to help others feel better

To build them up so they can find someone to love

Seems a noble life

A constant dagger in my heart

Watching, like playing a role in their life movie

Gets tiresome being me

Just me

But sometimes I feel these feelings....

CROWN

A tulip flower filled with tears

Like a field of nightmares

It abandoned love

Unto a thousand pieces

In wake the sun rose

Dried fears

Loved and replaced tears

It set on a meadows view

On still plains it glows souls

On starry nights

Darkness within light

Memories fade

The sun my comfort

A crown now filled with light

My delight

But we all have these layers within us...

LAYERS

She had been through hell which created many ugly layers

The only one to be brave enough to remove them would need to be

special

Years of pain and disappointment covered her from head to toe

The scars of untrusting were like an endless vast darkened sea in a storm

The unjustifiable effect had changed her view, intolerance and

skepticism

Unloved, it created vast walls as high and as far as the eye could see

But in all those layers, far below and hidden was peace and love

Neatly tucked away in the innermost foundations of her creation

Someone brave enough would peel them to reveal all that was hidden

Trust kept secretly in wait

A love that emanated from the core, set free

Those layers were endless, but love was bigger and created peace itself

Those layers looked like imperfections

For where in the confines of those layers a treasure

Waiting to give it away to the worthy warrior who refused to give up and decided to stay

Some layers we have inside are like the daisy's many petals, which are dark and never get to fully catch the light...

CLOSET FULL OF DEAD FLOWERS

I cry in dark nights,

In dim lights and on the edge of losing my sanity

I hide my darkness in closets no one can see

The fragments of bitter tasting dark chocolate surfaces on my tongue

Holding back rising words, like bile

Screaming in the darkness, these emptied secrets collected

Feeling numbed and lifeless from an abscessed loveless quest

My closet filled, devoid of care and the exterior bare

I hide in plain sight for all to view

Yet deep inside you decay from lies hidden

Wearing the mask of someone I thought I knew

I know not which is worse

But the scars burn from the twisted knife in my chest

And as the sin sets in, those crumbled, ground down to dust

All of what's left is me,

A closet filled with these dead flowers

But as I reflected on my life I realized how much I was comparative to a rose...

ROSE

When newly in bloom, I was as beautiful and as innocent as a rose

The morning dew twinkled on my young skin

I danced like confidence

But I was cut down from earliest of beginnings

Became dark and unforgiving from all of life's deceiving

Petals from my old life shed like a dying flower

Formed by a new harder and thicker skin

My will strong but never did I bloom the way I was meant

Protective thorns stuck out kept me safe

For I could not give the sun a chance to give me light

And it frightened me

Because I wouldn't be able to take another of that kind of bloom

Messing with my thoughts it burned my leaves

I withdrew from you

Must go before I would be ripped out by my root

So I stabbed first so it would lessen the blow

Questioning, testing to see who was worthy

To see who would stay

But you didn't, I was replaced

I was nothing more than a flower to cut

Admire, a throw away

Oh but to be a flower unencumbered and free, but that was not to be...

UNENCUMBERED

Disconnected, rejected

Not obsessed with

But truth be told lately, I'm a mess with

So invested in

Love

This arm's length

Connection, affection

Wanting more

Distance is a whore

Fighting isolation

Keeping score

Waiting for?

Hope is a chore

Futures order

Bitterness

Creeps in like darkness

Tortures souls

Cont'd

Covers me

Swallowed me whole

It's so hard to see

I've fallen deep

Happy end?

Not sure I can make it there

Fighting despair

Does anyone out there care?

We are in this life cycle of a flower, wouldn't thought, wouldn't you agree?

THE CYCLE OF A FLOWER

In the soil

Dropped by a passing bird

I lay

Insignificant

I was trampled by people

Rain pushed me in deep

I lay in darkness

Dormant

I felt warmth coming from up above

Something pulled at me

The rain now nourished my soul

Growth

Small yet fragile

Pushing through

Needing to see where this warmth would take me

Determined

The hard soil was no match
I grew even still
The wind blew, but tougher I became
Decided

I bloomed in the warmth
Sun stroking my pedals
Beautiful I did not know
Content

My purpose I knew not
I stood for all to view
Seeing smiling faces pass by
Present

The days grew long
My pedals began to drop
One by one slowly
Dying

Lost in thought
I knew not
What my purpose was
Impermanence

The seeds fell
Beside me all around
I knew now what I was
Life

I made room for the new
My nutrients feed the seeds
New flowers grew
Cycle

With cycles of life comes a dream of love and lust for another who will feed our roots...

LOVE

Your purest emotion

Exposed; stood and naked for your affection

I'm in love; it's gone so deep

Starved for perfection

The darkness of not quite

To be loved in his reflection

Beauty of my skin; never satisfied

Raw soul connection I'm matching

Emotional; frustrating

A love awakened but never expressed

Animal attraction; Sexual tension

Feeling lost

Love in the absence of touch

An ever endless craving and desire for the

perfection of our match...

DAYDREAM

Sometimes when I daydream, I run my hands across your chest

Just to feel your muscles flex

I wrap my arms around your neck

Kiss those lips that call my name

Press my skin against your flesh

Stare into your eyes, I'm melted into you

Our sacred song became one

In this world of our own

Our touched souls drawn from a lifetime of pull

In your arms I am free

Comforted from your soul

In my dream you are always right next to me

*To Dream of you a new flower
not yet in bloom...*

THE WISH

If the kisses I'd give were vast like the grains of sand,

You'd never worry

If my love were like the stars in the sky, it would light the way to yours forever

If the sun and moon imprinted my love, the whole world would bend

If you knew the times I thought of you, there would be a loop of infinite number

If you knew it could be true, would you wish for me beside you?

Or Keep me buried, hidden in the dark

No one knew so the love was not mine, it was fantasy

I wish it'd to be real

Something I could touch

To sit upon its beauty in ecstasy, to feel a love that makes us quiver, just the sight and taste of...

TASTE

Ecstasy drips down my chin

You

every thought

On fire

A burning desire

The taste burned on my lip

So hard

Yet easy

To swallow every bit of you

The desire,

never enough

I'm hooked, roped in

Only see you

No other to ever compare to

Dreamy ebullience is forever

In love, connected

So addicting,

The taste of you

In these precious moments we are mesmerized, addicted to the eyes of our lover...

THE CHESTNUT STARE

I think about

Those eyes

Soft lines

Love lives there

Soul beauty

I've seen life, the dances in the iris

Reflective light with so many stories and insight

Deep in the depths of them

Vast as the sea

The strength in them

So clear

Without words

Those eyes encapsulated my desire

Engulfed my fire

Those chestnut eyes

Gives me wings and helps me fly

Sees in me what I cannot

Beauty that I have sought

A love mesmerized and I become lost

To see what you see I crave

To be what you think you see

I am not

The full bloom of love and all it

glitters it dances on the heart...

GLITTER

A love that I gave out

Loved me right back

It felt like the suns warmth on my skin

Off of waters that glisten

I was the glitter dancing in the sea

I mattered for once despite all my flaws and insecurity

I have never been here before

To shine like a gem in someone else's eye and feel secure

Even when my world was crushing me to oblivion

The love that shines and feeds my soul

I remember I am whole

He being him, just the presence

Not asking, not taking, just being

That made me believe I would survive and goodness exists

I could do it alone, because I am made by the pain that shaped me

But I don't want to

I glitter more when I'm around him

Ah, but to gaze into the heart of your love like a newly blossomed beautiful flower...

GAZE

Like a falling star breaking through the atmosphere

We gaze into darkness, still glowing galaxies

A million light years away, thought transcends souls

Awareness takes place

Stars shine brighter, when lost in space

Apart yet together, universal embrace

Darkness temporary, light returns

Love is our saving grace

On dark days when the sun is gone, our

flowers are powered by a smile so strong...

YOUR SMILE

You light up even my darkest place

You're not defined only to your tenderness and grace

But by the glow of your face

The light in your eyes

Those lips of kindness

The brows of a safe place

Your smile is my happy place

The smile that saved me in so many ways

The smile that resonates

An anchor

A guide

A beautiful place

When love is fully in bloom we expose ourselves to the vulnerabilities of flaws and raw emotion...

THE LETTER

I wrote you a letter, expressed in calligraphy

That every cherished moment, a gift for me

I gave you these sacred words whispered from an old soul

Written on scrolls of an ageless tradition

Vulnerable and exposed

A beautifully crafted piece of me

The veins of it bled out on bond paper, sparing nothing

Letter to shatter all doubt, love

Reply in wait for you

I left my heart on the page preview

But sometimes we have thorns that cut deep that prevent a love we wish to keep...

SHARDS

I've given freely what you choose to keep hidden

I've been hurt yet I have forgiven

Not for loving but for putting it into the wrong person

I gave out much more than he

Seems a bitter pill I have to keep ingesting

I love with my scars exposed

Yet he does not see my value

I've been put back together with shards of broken glass

Oh the pain of losing, fresh blood oozes

Always remains the same

I lose while he gains, feeds the ego while mine drains

The pain of loving deeply, you never become as you were

Torn apart by the one person whom you gave your heart

While my heart is in shards

But that is the life of a flower, so many sides to see...

PETALS

My life is like a flower

The petals have many sides to tell

Some petals show sadness

Some show and tell

Some cut down

Dead waste to preserve the core

Those petals that fell are me no more

You would not know me the winter before

My fallen petals are memories of who I used to be

Changing direction but always facing the suns truths

In winter dormant, a time to contemplate

In spring renewed, a time to awaken

Fresh curious petals of new

Ever learning, growing true

Constant evolution

A flower of forever learning

My petals of bruises that changed my view

Sometimes you just aren't the right flower to be picked just now, but we feel we must justify and explain...

EXPLAIN

I shouldn't have to explain

The life I've lived

The scars I wear, to justify

Too many mistakes

Too many lessons

The weight I bare

Even explained, would you care?

Your perspective

Your judgment

I will not explain

You cannot fathom

You did not live it, deaf ears

Explaining

Wasted air

So when the pain is seeping through the roots we build walls...

WALLS

Every day those walls stand so tall

No end in sight to see them fall

You won't let me in

Those walls so thick this skin

Brick by brick of hurt and pain

Deep down below the surface

Something happened to you

Year after year those bricks grew stronger

Too many times I try to break in

Won't you let me in?

I step back, fighting to be let in

I watch you from high in the tower

I'm going under

Watching you suffer

Please break these walls

I will wait

I am here to keep you safe

In absence of love we wait for the next flower of love to grow...

ABSENCE

In dreams we touch

The fabric of distance

When daylight dawns

Emptiness engulfed In clouds above

Our souls intertwine

Days and months

Strengthened in love

Bound by connection

The eye of my affection

I pray for dreams

Together no space

In absence I wait

In wait of this new love a flower must always remember still the importance of self- love...

HOME

I longed for home,

A place of my own

Searched high and low

Moved from place to place

But a hole remained

Decided others were the warmth I craved

Built bricks of trust and time

But they crumble just the same

You are not to blame

I am a home within my heart

Looked outward instead of what was plain

You're comfort is a place of love

But home is not a place that can be found

It is inside that carries us

In all my life's destinations

My core is solid and true

Inner being never left

Be thyself be true

IF we are rushed in growing we will find much distaste...

WEEDS

They grew with such force

Choking out flowers sources of life

Aggressive it takes over roots

It strangles views

Cuts off sunlight

Even cut down it begins to multiply

Poison its only option

Even then it changes place

Finding new things to take over

Just like the toxic trait of negative minds

Nothing good they will never find

A weed chokes out any good thought or idea

Stay far from this kind

They bleed poison on everything they see or hear

Making every option nothing but failed attempt

The company you keep is much the same

Trim out those weeds when first met

Otherwise they will fill the bed with nothing but ugliness

and dread

We must always nourish our roots first to

become strong...

ROOTS

I wandered this land as ever a soul could

Never leaving traces of where I stood

Having felt the ground beneath

I tried to implant roots to keep

Grounded in one place I thought it be best

Though I couldn't take root

For like the seasons, I changed most

What served me well, never lasting long

I craved new scenes, a new song

My roots have never been dug in deep

Never trusted to invest

I wondered for years until we met

Now all I want is to grow roots deep with you

Where ever you go, I will grow

Bound by love and your echo

I crave just peace with roots so strong

Forever invested and planted in

I wonder the world no more

I know my place

The root of it all

Your heart

But as I sway in the cool breeze the flower of my life, I look upon the sunshine with

a sense of ease...

DELICATE FLOWER

How delicate they sway in the wind

The laced look of white

By the side of the road they play

A delicate flower wild and free

Like the core of a woman who is true

She dances in the sunlight

Plays in the fields of life

Her fragrance casts smiles and joy

In summer heads turn, we always remember

She is strong, her roots dug deep in the concrete

Petals gather love and strength

And as gently as a fragile flower, in love she blooms

Standing tall, she just is

No boasting, no care at all

Fades gracefully in the fall

Remembered by all

I am not forgetting some of the main roots, so I give tribute to the heritage and give back some love for the place I've never been...

SCOTTISH THISTLES

Scotland's land and sea

Oh she be a bonnie beauty to be sure

The thistle, a hidden treasure

Purple hues of old, sprinkle the shore

Dancing near stones of Callanish

Fairies and folklore be told

Ye love of false men

Gazed upon the night

A midsummer breeze it gently blows

While the 'shining one' walks amongst

The only one who witness

The hills of Great Bernera, a shadow

The Loch Roag its ghosts do roam

Only the thistle knows its secrets

Among the crashing shore

Thank you for taking this journey, the life of a flower whose stems grow stronger with every word planted and sown, for all to see.

About the Author

Canadian author, illustrator who works for multiple publishing companies. She's a mom and owner of an online art shop, an avid blogger and more! Find all her books online.

Loved her poetry? Find her Metamorphosis Poetry book and get into an emotionally charged collection of poems.

www.ingramcontent.com/pod-product-compliance
Lightning Source LLC
Chambersburg PA
CBHW070337120526
44590CB00017B/2923